CHRISTMAS IN HAWAII

Mele Kalikimaka

Mele Kalikimaka is the thing to say
On a bright Hawaiian Christmas day.
That's the Island greeting that we send to you,
From the land where palm trees sway.
Here we know that Christmas will be green and bright.
The sun will shine by day and all the stars at night.
Mele Kalikimaka is Hawaii's way
To say a Merry Christmas,
A Merry, Merry Christmas, To you.

Lyrics by Alex Anderson   1949.

Mele Kalikimaka

Christmas in Hawaii

Narrative
by Julie Mehta

Mutual Publishing, Honolulu, Hawaii

Acknowledgements:

To Bonnie Friedman who originally compiled the
holiday recipes for her article "Holiday Ethnic Foods"
that appeared in the December 1989 issue of *Spirit of
Aloha* and to the originator of the recipes for allowing
their reprinting:
Betsy Cardoza- "Ozoni"
Ruthie De Ponte- "Chicken Long Rice," "Haupia"
Alan Ong- "Drunken Chicken"
Bobby Santos- "Malassadas"

To the Hawaii State Library System for compiling
"Christmas Carols in Hawaiian and English."

To Polygram/Island Music Publishing Group for
permission to reprint "Mele Kalikimaka" written
by Alex Anderson. Copyright © 1949 Polygram
International Publishing, Inc.

Previous Page: *Photo by Vernon Lee*

First Printing October 1991
123456789

ISBN#0-935180-68-0

Mutual Publishing
1127 11th Avenue
Honolulu, Hawaii 96816
Telephone (808) 924-7732
Fax (808) 734-4094

Printed in Korea

TABLE OF CONTENTS

To my parents and to all adults who make Christmas a special time for children, and especially to my mom, Joanne Mehta, who taught me to love and respect books.

J.M.

hristmas in Hawaii—when the warm *"Aloha"* greeting is replaced with *"Mele Kalikimaka,"* and the magic of the holiday season is nurtured by family gatherings, festivities, and religious observances. And when the combined ambiance of a semitropical setting and the multicultural diversity of Hawai'i's people contribute to a unique "traditional Hawaiian Christmas." ✿ For newcomers from colder climes experiencing Christmas in Hawai'i, there is the incongruity of a tropical sun gracing a Yuletide morning. If Christmas is measured only by cold weather, Hawai'i falls short. But if it is the spirit of the season that counts, then this holiday season finds no better welcome than in the islands. Downtown Honolulu has no shortage of evening joy as tens of thousands of small white lights twinkle in the night, draped around city poles, trees, fences, and buildings. The majestic 'Iolani Palace is unforgettable, outlined with its wonderful lights that burn from sunset to sunrise. Families outdo each other on elaborate house lights and yard decorations, some residential blocks actually staging competitions for the best and most unique

CHRISTMAS IN HAWAII

Christmas decorations. Nativity scenes, some even automated, have become extremely popular both at churches and private residences. 🦋 With Christmas morning usually bright and fair, the weather is perfect for outdoor activities. Just as Hawaiians celebrated the *makahiki* three hundred years before, contemporary islanders spend Christmas time surfing, swimming, canoeing, and playing in tournaments. Biathlons, triathlons, marathons, and other challenging competitions abound on Christmas Day and throughout the holiday season. 🦋 For Hawai'i's over 100,000 military personnel stationed far from their mainland homes, an island Christmas is a nostalgic season. On the military bases, the various units paint colorful billboards bearing holiday wishes. Pearl Harbor at night becomes a radiant sight with ships displaying multicolored Christmas lights strung from bow to mast to stern. The control towers at both Pearl Harbor Naval Base and neighboring Hickam Air Force Base are adorned with decorative lighting creating dazzling reflections in the harbor waters. At Schofield Barracks in Wahiawa, a specially selected Army family is given the honor of turning on the lights of the post Christmas tree. Then, "here comes Santa Claus," sitting atop a yellow fire engine, waving to the excited, shouting crowd of delighted youngsters who strain to get a sight of their very favorite person. 🦋 Thousands of sights and sounds and tastes make up a Hawaiian Christmas. Best of all, it is a time for island families to gather, to share their love and celebrate another year of aloha in Hawai'i. Torches and candles may have been replaced by electrical lights, but the Christmas spirit is everbright on the Hawaiian islands. *Mele Kalikimaka.*

onolulu had never seen a celebration quite like this one. The temporary Anglican church at Peleula had been elaborately decorated with cypress boughs cut from the mountains, an abundance of myrtle, orange boughs and beautiful native flowers. The altar,

THE FIRST CHRISTMAS IN HAWAII

festooned with verdant shrubs with large red cone-shaped berries, was graced with a large text reading, "The Word was made flesh." A silver candelabra lent by King Kamehameha IV cast a blazing light through the tiny church, which by midnight of Christmas Eve, 1862, was filled with joyous celebrants softly chanting the Litany in the native Hawaiian language. Thirty men and women received Holy Communion amid much singing and ritual. When the service ended at 1:00 AM, the battery at Punchbowl fired a salute as flaming tar barrels cascaded down the crater's rim. The first official observance of Christmas in the Hawaiian islands had begun. ❦ In ancient times, the people of old had celebrated the abundance of the harvest and Lono, the god of peace, with the *makahiki*, a lengthy holiday season of special feasts and games. It was a time when goodwill prevailed and thanksgiving was revered. When the first European voyagers came to Hawai'i, they often celebrated Christmas in the islands, sometimes exchanging gifts and festivities with the Native Hawaiians. The first recorded Christmas in Hawai'i was on December 25, 1786, when Captain Nathaniel Portlock of the *King George* (and Captain George Dixon of the *Queen Charlotte*) exchanged Yuletide pleasantries with Hawaiians at Waimea Bay, Kaua'i. On Christmas Eve the crew enjoyed roast pig and sea-pie and "offered our Christmas libations in punch, mixed with the juice of the coconut, toasting our friends and mistresses in bumpers of this liquor, which perhaps, pleased more on account of its novelty than from any other circumstance." ❧ On Christmas morning, over a hundred women carrying children in their arms gathered among the foreign captains, each child receiving a small gift with delight. Later that day, the chief of the village reciprocated the presents with a present of hogs and vegetables. The first staff Christmas party and exchange of Yuletide gifts had taken place in Hawai'i with evidently much mutual pleasure. ❧ In the intervening years, foreigners of all backgrounds and religious persuasions visited the Hawaiian islands, some remaining among the native people and introducing their own religious holidays and customs. King Kamehameha the Great celebrated Christmas Eve 1817 with an English visitor on his ship in Honolulu harbor. The next day, the English and Kamehameha enjoyed a large native *pa'aina*, feast, on shore. Early Catholic settlers in Honolulu, such as the venerable Don Francisco de Paula Marin no doubt held private Christmas observances for their families and friends as did British and American sandalwood merchants. ❧ When the brig *Thaddeus* arrived in Hawai'i in the spring of 1820 bearing the pioneer company of American Protestant missionaries, the religious nature of Christmas celebration would take a new turn. Tracing their religious convictions to their conservative New England Puritan church, these congregationalist missionaries believed that only those religious observances specifically set forth in the Bible should be celebrated. While Thanksgiving in November, gift-giving on New Year's Eve, and feasting on the Fourth of July were observed by the missionaries, Christmas celebrations were considered a Catholic ritual not condoned by the Bible. Consequently, the day of the Lord's birth was observed with quiet prayer and "business as usual." ❧ The powerful influence of the early missionary church prevailed in Hawai'i through half a century despite the later arrival of Catholics, Methodists, and secular Americans who were embracing Christmas on the mainland as a joyous family celebration complete with home decorations, Christmas trees, and St. Nick. At Washington Place on December 25, 1858, Mrs. John Dominis hosted a Christmas party that included a prominent, gaily decorated tree, a Santa Claus, and other customs that were quickly becoming Victorian traditions in England. ❄ Even the children of missionaries were touched by this changing climate of Christmas joy. Punahou, the mission school in Manoa Valley, staged a Christmas day picnic for the students in 1847, although the faculty stressed it was in anticipation of New Year's Day. Perhaps the staunchest of the missionary leaders, Reverend Hiram Bingham, noted in his journals for Christmas 1841 that his children had hung out their stockings with the "ridiculous notion" that Santa Claus would leave them some small gifts! Needless to say, their stockings the next day were bare. ❄ With the ascension of Kamehameha IV, Alexander Liholiho, to the throne in 1854, the young King and his part-English bride Queen Emma would lean away from Puritanism and toward British traditions. As early as 1857 the King proclaimed December 25th Thanksgiving Day in Hawai'i, an edict that allowed foreigners and natives of all faiths to honor the day, each in their own way. Finally in 1862, His Majesty openly embraced the Anglican faith, inviting a branch of the church to be introduced to the islands.

Receiving baptism in the church, Kamehameha IV then proclaimed that Christmas, December 25, would become an official holiday in the Hawaiian islands. ❄ It was His Majesty King Kamehameha IV who had donated much of the floral decorations for the Peleula church services on Christmas Eve. He also translated into Hawaiian the Litany which was chanted. Following the beautiful display of Punchbowl crater aglow with lava-like flames, His Majesty then led an unusual procession of celebrants through downtown Honolulu. Twenty torches made of *kukui* wood and coconut fibers dipped in tar and standing eight feet tall followed His Majesty as the procession walked down Fort and King Streets. Green candles were burning along the parade route with onlookers and marchers singing Christmas carols. Gathering at the fountain courtyard at the King's Palace, the processioners, numbering in the thousands, delighted in the igniting of fireworks and rockets shot into the air with the great shout of the crowd. At this point, as one reveler remembers, "We sang the grand old carol 'Good King Winceslaus' (sic); and after a glass of champagne punch we made the air right with the National Anthem, and another round of protracted Hurrahs, and so to bed." ❄ *Mele Kalikimaka* had forever become a part of life in the Hawaiian islands.

For several nights before Christmas Day, thousands of Oahuans drive downtown for what has become a Honolulu tradition—the holiday celebration at Honolulu Hale, where lights abound in a surrounding 16-block area filled with hundreds of sparkling, glittering trees and festively lit office buildings. 🌺 The focal point is the beautiful decorated Christmas Tree that stands prominently in front of Honolulu Hale. The lighting of this 50-foot tall Norfolk pine strung with 225 strands of lights and the accompanying Christmas musical program are the highlight of the downtown celebration. Inside Honolulu Hale, dozens of decorated Christmas trees create an enchanted forest. Standing guard are large wooden soldiers and animated figures that entice children of all ages. The favorite is the twelve-foot Hawaiian St. Nick who is "cooling off" with a dip of his toe in Honolulu Hale's fountain, his hand giving the characteristic "shaka" sign that is the island's way to say, "Howzit?" 🌺 From the night flaming tar barrels rolled down Punchbowl in 1862 to Honolulu's present day festival of lights, the island tradition of setting the night aglow has been perpetuated.

HONOLULU
CITY LIGHTS
A CHRISTMAS MAGIC

Opposite: *Toy soldiers stand on guard near the majestic archways of Honolulu Hale where a forest of Christmas trees create holiday magic.*
Photo: Peter French

Above: *Santa's reindeer lunch by an artificial waterfall at a downtown Honolulu intersection. With the cooperation of developers, the city has been able to create and beautify many midtown open spaces. Most feature running water and shade trees, imaginatively lighted for the Yule season.*
Photo: Doug Peebles

Opposite: *Hawaii's friendliest Santa Claus epitomizes the aloha spirit with his "shaka" sign in front of the Honolulu Hale fountain. This little tyke is trying to get a last look before going home.*
Photo: Vernon Lee

THE DILLINGHAM TRANSPORTATION BUILDING

Opposite: *A couple waits for a cab in front of the Dillingham Transportation Building on Bishop Street in downtown Honolulu after an evening of holiday merrymaking.*
Photo: Doug Peebles

Above: *White reindeer graze on the lawn of Washington Place, the governor's official residence in Honolulu. Can you find Rudolph?*
Photo: Doug Peebles

Following: *The lawns of the Board of Water Supply on Beretania Blvd. in downtown Honolulu annually present animated electric displays of lights. Suspended Hibiscus flowers and umbrellas open and close as electric light rain clouds shower on these figures.*
Photo: Doug Peebles

Above: *Everyone joins in the excitement of the season. This dazzling **lei** of lights is on a downtown Honolulu parking garage. Flowers light in sequence throughout the night. Auto traffic is restricted in the center of the capital to encourage family sightseeing on foot or in carriages.*
Photo: Peter French

Opposite: *Two Honolulu newspapers join in providing Christmas magic at the downtown intersection of South Street and Kapiolani Boulevard, opposite City Hall. The papers share presses and delivery services in an unusual exemption from U.S. anti-monopoly laws.*
Photo: Peter French

Above: *The Mayor's Christmas tree in front of Honolulu Hale, the City Hall, stands Island proud among the palm trees following its ceremonial joint lighting by the Governor and Mayor. Several thousand colored lights decorate trees on the lawn and lining the nearby streets.*
Photo: Vernon Lee

Opposite: *A star-burst of light in the majestic painted night sky glimmers SEASONS GREETINGS from a city construction crane.*
Photo: Doug Peebles

Opposite: *This Waikiki apartment condominium cherishes its reputation as the Ala Wai Boulevard's "best dressed" for Christmas. The rivalry among apartment buildings for the honor is informal and friendly, but highly competitive.*
Photo: Peter French

Above: *Tripler Army Hospital's familiar pink shaded building, covered with lights during the holiday, can be seen for miles around. During the day a giant red and yellow "Season's Greetings" sign keeps the Christmas message flowing.*
Photo: Vernon Lee

Following: *The shimmering magic of Christmas comes to Pearl Harbor as the winter sun sets on the U.S. Navy's Pacific Fleet home port.*
Photo: Doug Peebles

Above: *Hawaii's legendary* **menehune**, *"the little people," appear to have trimmed these Norfolk Island pine trees on a hillside with garlands and Christmas ornaments. A Windward Oahu landmark, Mt. Olomana, rises in the background.*
Photo: *Doug Peebles*

Opposite: *How does Santa Claus arrive in Hawaii? By canoe, of course! Every year he comes ashore at the Outrigger Canoe Club in Waikiki. Here he can be seen paddling among the tropical foliage.*
Photo: *Doug Peebles*

Opposite: *The firemen of the Makiki station in midtown Honolulu annually wish all a* **Mele Kalikimaka** *("Merry Christmas") and Happy New Year. The Makiki neighborhood's Christmas parade always includes their shining red fire engines, complete with sirens and flashing lights.* Photo: *Doug Peebles*

Above: *Henry Lutz continues a family tradition! His Hawaii Kai home decorations include Santa arriving at the Lutz's front door in a canoe, pulled by harnessed dolphins. Candy canes and candles border the driveway.* Photo: *Vernon Lee*

Following: *A tropical holiday paradise in Waimanalo Oahu, bursting with colored light, harvests glowing palm trees and magical electric enchantments.* Photo: *Doug Peebles*

Above Left: *A dapper Santa displays his designer Aloha wear to shoppers in Paia, Hawaii's wind-surfing capital. (This is where Santa spends his vacations!) Photo: G. Brad Lewis*

Top Right: *Brilliant red poinsettias—a popular decorative shrub in Hawaii— fortify this hillside in front of a Kona home. Photo: G. Brad Lewis*

Above Right: *A Nativity scene among the* **hapu'u** *ferns of Makawao, Maui. Photo: G. Brad Lewis*

You can find cozy fireplaces in Hawaii. This hearth at a bed-and-breakfast lodge near Kilauea Volcano on the Big Island, built in 1938, has coins and mementos from all over the world embedded in its walls.
Photo: Peter French

Following: *Shops and a giant fairy-lighted monkey-pod tree brighten the evening in Koloa Town, on the Island of Kauai. Hawaii's first successful sugar plantation was at Koloa, now the focal point of a steadily expanding visitor-destination and resort area.*
Photo: Peter French

sland style permeates all aspects of holiday celebrations in Hawai'i giving a distinctive Mele Kalikimaka flavor to ornaments, decorations, gifts and even table settings. 🌺 The traditional haku lei is combined with the Christmas wreath to produce green and red floral displays seen nowhere else. Festive floral decorations using the Hawaiian poinsettia or Bird of Paradise are found everywhere. Hawaiian angels made from coconut fibers adorn family Christmas trees while green fern centerpieces spell out the word *"Aloha"* on dining room tables. 🌺 Imaginative Asian traditions turn the Japanese bonsai plant into a miniature Christmas tree with perfect, tiny red Christmas bulbs. 🌺 Portuguese and Filipinos of Hawai'i display distinctive Christmas decorations, foods, and songs from their homelands. 🌺 Christmas craft fairs abound with native koa wood picture frames, shell jewelry boxes, tie-dyed and silkscreened garbs of distinctive Hawaiian themes, as well as other artistic creations reflecting island themes. 🌺 Hawaiian Christmas dinner tables offer unparalleled feasts of traditional holiday fare alongside local ethnic dishes of all description.

CHRISTMAS FLAVORS HAWAIIAN STYLE

Opposite: *The traditional Christmas trees are given the Hawaiian touch. Ornaments that adorn the tree, (symbols of the islands and Aloha life), are incorporated into the decorations. Dolphins, pineapples, Hawaiian dressed angels can be seen hanging from the limbs of Christmas trees. Photo: Rae Huo*

Above: *Coconut-husk angels in the lobby of the Mauna Kea Beach Hotel on the Big Island remind guests and staff of the Christmas season. Luxury resorts and humbler bed-and-breakfast* *lodges annually accommodate thousands escaping winter weather on the U.S. Main-land, Canada, Northern Europe and the Far East. Photo: Peter French*

Opposite: *The Mauna Kea Beach Hotel's proud Christmas tree, decorated with symbols of Hawaii and her people, greets both visitors and Big Islanders. Photo: Peter French*

Opposite: *City employees take pride in decorating the Christmas trees. Creativity, teamwork, and a little Yuletide magic create the lighted Christmas trees that citizens throng to see.*
Photo: Peter French

Above: *This Christmas tree at Honolulu Hale, Honolulu's City Hall, wears some decorations peculiar to Hawaii. Among those visible are. . . (can anyone identify?)*
Photo: Doug Peebles

Following: *Christmas lights, ornaments, and crowds are annual delights at Honolulu Hale. Not only are trees illuminated with hundreds of tiny lights but the surrounding lawns are given over to story-book characters made by city employees to delight strollers.*
Photo: Peter French

Above Left: *A majestic King Protea blossom and vibrant Bird-of-Paradise flowers make up this regal and exotic wreath designed by "stylists" Greg Howell and Steven Minkowski. Photo: Steven Minkowski*

Top Right: *A very country Hawaiian Santa clad in a farmer's shirt, garland lei with one pretty red Hibiscus and with his burlap bag of goodies, contributes to this wreath's Aloha ambiance. Photo: Doug Peebles*

Above Right: *Protea flowers from "up-country" Maui become a Hawaiian wreath. Photo: Rae Huo*

Anthuriums, orchids, torch ginger and papertree bark are used in this fabulous Christmas wreath.
Photo: Steve Minkowski

Following: *In Hawaii, Christmas decorations, crafts and gifts reflect the local flavor with special island touches.*
Photo: Rae Huo

Opposite: *A Hawaiian-style holiday* **luau** *includes (clockwise from upper left): squid-meat appetizer,* **lomi** *salmon, chicken long rice,* **haupia** *coconut pudding,* **poi,** *Hawaiian salt, onion,* and pit-baked **kalua** pig, *prepared by Ruthie DePonte, Michale W. Ham and Naomi Enomoto of the Pukalani (Maui) Terrace Country Club.*
Photo: Steven Minkowski

Above: *Portuguese Christmas dinner (clockwise from upper left):* **vinha d'alhos** *pork,* **malassadas** *("doughnut holes"), salad, and* **vinha d'alhos** *chicken, prepared by Bobby Santos, Chris Speere and food service students at Maui Community College.*
Photo: Steven Minkowski

Above: *Japanese New Year morning meal: (clockwise from upper left):* **Kuromame** *(beans with chestnuts),* **sashimi,** *fish eggs, fish cake and baked fish, prepared by Betsy Cardoza of Tokyo Tei Restaurant in Wailuku, Maui.*
Photo: Steven Minkowski

Opposite: *Chinese New Year dinner (clockwise from upper right): "drunken chicken,"* **lau hon jai,** *and fried* **yee mein,** *prepared by Alan Ong and Eric Dela Cruz of Ming Yuen Restaurant in Kahului, Maui.*
Photo: Steven Minkowski

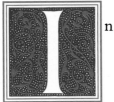I n Hawai'i, Christmas season is a time for local high school marching bands playing holiday tunes, followed by flower-bedecked fire trucks, Hawaiian pa'u riders on horseback, *paniola* or cowboys with festive holiday wreaths about their hats, pretty cheerleaders, Boy Scouts and Girl Guides, and the favored guest of honor, Santa Claus. The arrival of St. Nick in Hawai'i is always a surprise, especially since he has been known to visit the islands by unusual modes of transportation, including traditional Hawaiian canoes as well as helicopters. 🌺 Special Christmas programs are found throughout the islands—including concerts of the Honolulu Boy Choir, the Hawai'i Youth Symphony, the Honolulu Symphony, Chorus' performances of Handel's *Messiah*, and renditions of the Nutcracker ballet. An experience is the Christmas Eve evening church service at historic Kawaiahao Church. 🌺 And what would Christmas be without gifts? Since the first exchange of gifts between Europeans and Hawaiians in 1786, islanders show an unsurpassed enthusiasm for gift-giving. Hawaiian generosity combined with the Asian sense of reciprocal gift-giving has fueled the island passion for Christmas presents.

ISLAND CELEBRATIONS AND GIFTS

Opposite: *Flags and lady Pa'u riders are always favorites in Honolulu's annual Aloha Bowl Parade through the city center.* Photo: Doug Peebles

Above: *Girls in green and red do a movable hula on a float in the Kaneohe community Christmas parade. The hula is based on authentic Hawaiian culture, considerably standardized these days and taught in many studios. The performances at the annual Merrie Monarch festival in Hilo are watched by the entire State, to the neglect of network football. Photo: Doug Peebles*

Opposite: *The colorful leis, hats and gowns of three regal* **pa'u** *riders from Honolulu's Waimanalo neighborhood catch the festive spirit of the season. Parades are an integral part of Hawaii's Christmas. The* **pa'u** *skirts worn by these women are holdovers from the days of the Hawaiian monarchy of the nineteenth century. Photo: Doug Peebles*

Opposite: *Honolulu's nationally televised Aloha Bowl Parade has it all — including graceful dancers and gigantic balloons floating over palm-lined Waikiki streets. An all-star football game between teams of college players chosen from throughout the United States follows in Aloha Stadium overlooking Pearl Harbor.* Photo: Doug Peebles

Above: *"Let's try that again! All together this time."* Photo: Doug Peebles

Above: *Here come the Kaneohe community cyclists! They are all part of the Yuletide excitement. Kaneohe Town occupies a broad coastal plain, with few elevations, so that cycling is popular. Crossing the island to Honolulu proper, however, involves steep climbs and a series of tunnels.*
Photo: Doug Peebles

Opposite: *A worried-looking Santa Claus bows to onlookers as he floats above Kalakaua Avenue in Waikiki. Hotel and airline workers generally handle the balloon's lines. Residents and visitors alike line the two-mile parade route stretching from Fort DeRussy to Diamond Head.*
Photo: Doug Peebles

Opposite: *Downtown Honolulu's Mission Houses Museum offers ukulele music appropriate to Christmas during its annual craft fair. These ladies accompany themselves on the ukulele.*

Within the Mission Houses complex is the first western-style structure erected in Hawaii, assembled from pre-cut timber shipped around Cape Horn from Boston.
Photo: Doug Peebles

Above: ***Tutus*** *("aunties"), elegant in crimson* **muumuu** *gowns and festive flower leis, are honored at the Kaneohe community's Christmas festivities in Windward Honolulu. Hawaii's older*

citizens of all ethnic backgrounds play an important part in community life, particularly in the upbringing of children.
Photo: Doug Peebles

Above: *A magical scene,*
adapted from the classical
Nutcracker *ballet is performed*
Hawaiian style by the
University of Hawaii-Hilo
drama students.
Photo: G. Brad Lewis

Opposite: *Hilo dancers*
bring excitement and a sense
of awe to this jellyfish scene.
Photo: G. Brad Lewis

Above Left: *The Christmas craft fair at Thomas Square in central Honolulu is an annual delight. These exquisite Hawaiian angels are decked in flower leis, **muumuus**, and traditional Hawaiian garb.*
Photo: Doug Peebles

Top Right: *A wreath maker is involved in her craft at Honolulu's historic Kawaihao Church annual crafts fair.*
Photo: Doug Peebles

Above Right: *Hawaii's vibrant colors are everywhere at the holiday craft fairs in midtown Thomas Square.*
Photo: Doug Peebles

Getting ready for The
Honolulu Advertiser's
Jingle Bell Run — One of
Oahu's most festive events
that attracts over 3,000
participants who wear jingle
bells (what else?) on their
costumes and shoes. The
spotted great dane is real —
he's not a runner in disguise.
Photo: Doug Peebles

Following: *The enormous
poinsettias suspended above
the mall's outdoor stage add
to the wonder and excitement
of holiday shopping at Ala
Moana Center.*
Photo: Gary Hofheimer

Above: "Here's looking at you, Santa." The Ala Moana Shopping Center's Christmas centerpiece is an annual marvel of engineering as it is brought out of its off-season storage and hoisted into position over the central court of this sprawling outdoor mall. Photo: Peter French

Opposite: The Ala Moana Center's stage has nonstop entertainment through December. Stunning red Christmas poinsettias back the garlanded slack-key guitar and ukulele performers.

The slack-key guitar is a Hawaiian development largely responsible for the characteristic "sliding" sound of Island music. Photo: Peter French

Christmas is a day for families and friends, parades and dinners, fireworks and gifts. It is also and will always be a special day for *keiki*, the children. What has really changed from that day in 1786 when Hawaiian children received small gifts from Captains Dixon and Portlock and vividly expressed their glee in radiant eyes and smiles? Who can ever forget the sight of Hawai'i's golden children seeing their first

CHRISTMAS' SPECIAL PEOPLE

Christmas tree, wondering what was in that oddly shaped present and waiting impatiently as father and mother handed everyone their gifts so that they could rip off the wrapping to find the surprise inside? ❧ Christmas begins as a childhood memory that continues through the years to remind us of the value of charity, generosity, love, and peace. In the multi-ethnic faces of Hawai'i's children, the true spirit of Christmas continues to live. Island traditions and customs have been handed down through the generations, and are passed on to the *keiki*, recognizing that in them, the island celebration of Christmas is perpetuated. To the children of Hawai'i, and to the child in all of our hearts, *pumehana aloha nui loa. Mele Kalikimaka.*

Opposite: Look at me! No reason to get up when among friends dressed in such unusual Christmas attire. Photo: P.A. Scully

Above: *Young aspiring actors about to go on stage for their school Christmas play, nervously knowing that mom and dad are eagerly awaiting their performance.*
Photo: Doug Peebles

Opposite: *What was Santa promising when the photographer interrupted him? At almost every shopping mall in the State, Santa Claus waits to accept wish lists from children—and often to pose with them for a family photo. He also gets to ride in countless community parades.*
Photo: Vernon Lee

Above: *These young
participants in a Nativity-
scene float in the Kaneohe
Town Christmas Parade
changed character quickly
when they spotted a friend
among the spectators.
Photo: Doug Peebles*

Opposite: *Who is this
pretty Princess reigning over
the Christmas parade at the
ranching community of
Waimea, on the Island of
Hawaii? Interestingly,
Waimea has an alternate
name, "Kamuela," given it*

*nearly two hundred years
ago by local **paniolo** cow-
boys in honor of Samuel
(Kamuela in Hawaiian)
Parker, founder of today's
huge Parker Ranch.
Photo: Peter French*

Above Left: *This three year old future artist takes time out of asking Santa for a train set to pose for a photo.*
Photo: Phyllis Gonzalez

Top Right:
The perfect angel.
Photo: Doug Peebles

Above Right: *"Pretty comfortable seats, huh, sis?" Spectators at Honolulu's annual Jingle Bell Run.*
Photo: Vernon Lee

*Christmas is a special time
for all. These girls are
awaiting their turn to
"go on" for their school's
Christmas program.
Photo: Peter French*

Opposite: *Some future karate black belts, just in from the North Pole, participate in the Waimea community parade on Hawaii's Big Island. Photo: Peter French*

Above: *Christmas means school pageants in Hawaii, too. These three suburban Honolulu preschool "reindeer" pose for a publicity shot while awaiting their turn in a Yule tableau. Photo: Doug Peebles*

Following: *Hula dancers add a special Hawaiian character to the Kaneohe community Christmas parade. Photo: Doug Peebles*

TIGERS

Opposite: *Hawaii's pleasant weather allures children to avoid bulky winter clothing. Shorts and T-shirts do fine for these fighting tigers.*
Photo: Doug Peebles

Above: *Snow in Waikiki! It's manmade but no less exciting for this youngster making her first snowball.*
Photo: Doug Peebles

Following: *Alas, there is real snow for Hawaii's kids to play with at Christmas. Unfortunately, it may be hard to reach. One can see snow atop the 13,000 foot summit of Mauna Kea. Look closely for the "Boogie Board" skier just to the left of the Canadian-French-Hawaii observatory.*
Photo: Peter French

CHRISTMAS CAROLS
(Translation in Hawaiian)

Hark! The Herald Angels Sing
Hamau E Na Kanaka

🎵 Hark! the her-ald an-gels sing,
Ha-amu e na ka-na-ka,
"Glo-ry to the new-born King;
Me-le mai na a-ne-la,
Peace on earth, and mer-cy mild
Ei-a ke 'Lii ha-nau hou
God and sin-ners rec-on-ciled!"
E hoo-na-ni ae ou-kou!
Joyful, all ye na-tions, rise,
Ma-lu no ko la-lo nei,
Join the tri-umph of the skies;
E hau o-li hoo-mai-kai!
With th' an-gel-ic hosts pro-claim,
Ke A-ku-a, ko ke ao,
"Christ is born in Beth-le-hem!"
Ku-i-ka-hi pu la-kou,
Hark! the her-ald an-gels sing,
Ke A-ku-a, ko ko ao,
"Glo-ry to the new-born King."
Ku-i-ka-hi pu la-kou.

Away In The Manger
He Kapu Hanai

🎵 A-way in a man-ger, no crib for His bed,
He ka-pu ha-na-i oi-a ka mo-e
The lit-tle Lord Je-sus laid down His sweet head.
No ke ka-mai-ki no hi-a-mo-e ai
The stars in the sky looked down where He lay,
Na-na mai la na ho-ku mai-lu-na mai.
The lit-tle Lord Je-sus, a-sleep on the hay.
Ia Ie-su ka Ha-ku o mo-e lai ana.

O Come, All Ye Faithful
Hoonanikakou Iaia

🎵 O come, all ye faith-ful,
E he-le mai ou-kou ke
   joy-ful and tri-um-phant,
   po-e ma-na'o i-'o
O come-ye, o come-ye to Beth-le-hem;
E he-le hau-o-li'i Be-te-le-hema,
Come and be-hold Him,
Hele mai a i-ke
   born the King of an-gels;
   I ka Mo-i ha-nau hou
O come, let us a-dore Him,
Hoo-na-ni ka-kou Ia-ia,
O come let us a-dore Him,
Hoo-na-ni ka-kou Ia-ia,
   Christ, - the Lord!
   Kris-to ka Haku.

It Came Upon The Midnight Clear
He Po Laelae Ka Hiki 'Na Mai

It came up-on the mid-night clear,
'Ka po lae-lae ka hi-ki'na mai
That glo-rious song of old,
Ia mea-le o-li nei
From an-gels bend-ing near the earth
Mai na a-ne-la a i ke ao
To touch their harps of gold;
Hoo-ka-ni ma-i la-kou
"Peace on the earth - good will to men,
He ma-lu, he-a-lo-ha no
From heav'n's all gra-cious King."
Mai ka-Ma-ku-a mai
The world in sol-emn still-ness lay
He me-ha ma ke ao a-pau
To hear the an-gels sing,
A lo-he no la-kou.

And ev-er o'er its Ba-bel sounds
Hoo-ka-ni no a lo-he ia
The bless-ed an-gels sing.
Ka leo a na a-ne-la.

Still through the clo-ven skies they come,
Mai lo-ko ma-i o ke ao
With peace-ful wings un-furled,
A we-he ae na-e-heu
And still their heav'n-ly mu-sic floats
A o na me-le ke o mai la
O'er all the wea-ry world;
I ke ao lu-hi nei
A-bove its sad and low-ly plains
Ma-lu-na a-e o ka ho-nua
They bend on hov-'ring wing,
Ku-lo-u mai no la-kou

LOCAL FLAVORS

Portuguese Christmas Recipe

by Bobby Santos

Malassadas

6 cups flour
1 cup sugar
5 eggs, beaten
1 cup milk
1/3 cup melted butter, cooled
2 1/2 tsp. yeast
1 tsp. salt
1 cooked potato, mashed
1 cup water

Dissolve yeast in 1/3 cup lukewarm water and 1 tsp. sugar. Mix flour, remainder of sugar and salt together in a large bowl. Add milk, remainder of water and potato to flour mixture. Add butter, eggs, and yeast mixture. Mix and let rest for two hours, covered, in a warm place. Scoop rounded spoonfuls into hot fat. Deep-fry until golden brown. Roll in granulated sugar. Makes approximately 24- 2 oz. malassadas.

Hawaiian Christmas Recipes

by Ruthie De Ponte

Chicken Long Rice

2 lbs. chicken thighs, deboned
1 clove garlic, minced
2-inch long piece of fresh ginger, minced
1/2 tsp. Hawaiian salt
1 tsp. ground black pepper
5 cups water
1 Tbsp. shoyu
2 Tbsp. white wine
1 package long rice (soak in water)

In a pot, fry chicken, garlic, ginger, salt and pepper until chicken meat is cooked through. Add water, shoyu and wine. Bring to a boil. Add long rice and simmer until it becomes transparent. Serves 6.

Haupia

1 can (12 oz.) frozen coconut milk
4 to 6 Tbsp. sugar
4 to 6 Tbsp. cornstarch
3/4 cup water

Thaw coconut milk. Combine sugar and cornstarch; stir in water and blend well. Stir sugar mixture into thawed coconut milk; cook and stir over low heat until thickened. Pour into 8 inch square pan and chill until firm. Cut into 2 inch squares.

Chinese New Year Recipe

by Alan Ong

Drunken Chicken

3 to 4 lb. frying chicken (whole)
1 bottle shaosing wine
8 oz. piece fresh ginger
4 oz. green onions (whole, trimmed)
8 oz. ebi (dried shrimp)
1 lb. spareribs
1 cup light soy sauce
sugar (to taste)
salt (to taste)
1 cup vegetable oil
2 cups chicken broth
1/4 cup each Chinese peas, sliced bamboo,
sliced carrots, Chinese black mushrooms

🌿 Rub chicken with 1/2 cup of the soy sauce until the skin looks dark brown in color. Fry the whole chicken in oil until skin is cooked and is dark in color. Remove from pan. Drain. Set aside. In the bottom of a large pot, place the spareribs, ginger, green onions, ebi, shaosing wine, chicken broth, salt and sugar. Lay the chicken on top of the ribs and simmer for two hours, covered. Baste and check for tenderness every 20 minutes. When chicken is cooked remove from pot and place in a large, deep serving bowl. Pour the excess liquid (without ribs) into another pot. Add the Chinese peas, bamboo, carrots and black mushrooms. Cook until tender. Add a little corn-starch to thicken the sauce and pour over the chicken. Serves 4.

Japanese New Year Recipe

by Betsy Cardoza

Ozoni (traditional soup)

1 quart water
1/3 cup bonito (dried fish) shavings
1 piece kelp (2 inch by 2 inch)
dash of salt
dash of shoyu
sliced- daikon (Japanese radish), carrot, lotus,
    dasheen (a starchy vegetable like a potato),
    mizuna (a Japanese cabbage)- tradition dictates
    that the slices be round for the New Year
mochi (Japanese dumplings traditionally served on
New Year)

🌿 Add bonito shavings, kelp, salt and shoyu to water and bring to a boil. Boil slowly for 1/2 hour. Add daikon, carrot, lotus, dasheen. Add mizuna and mochi last. As soon as mochi is soft, serve. Serves 4.

🌿 *All Oriental ingredients are available in Oriental food sections of major supermarkets or Asian markets.*

Christmas Notes

About the Author

After growing up in California, Julie Mehta graduated as an ensign from the U.S. Coast Guard Academy. Her first tour of duty was aboard the Coast Guard cutter *Jarvis*, homeported at Honolulu. ❦ Between patrols to and from Alaska, and occasional U.S. mainland assignments, Miss Mehta discovered the uniqueness of the Hawaiian Christmas from which came the idea for this book, done in collaboration with noted island photographers. ❦ Lieut. (JG) Julie Mehta, now in her second Hawai'i tour, is with the U.S. Coast Guard's Readiness Branch at Honolulu where she is an exercise planner and aide to the Commander 14th Coast Guard District.

Art Direction
by Leo Gonzalez

Design
by Darlene Koning Tokunaga

Typesetting
by HonBlue

Editorial Assistance
by Glen Grant

Corporate Liason
by Galyn Wong

Text and Captions:
C.G. Bembo Roman and Italic

Initial Ornamental Caps:
Historic Alphabets and Initials,
Woodcut and Ornamental;
by Carol Belanger Grafton;
Dover Publications, Inc.

Printed and Bound in Korea

Mele Kalikimaka

To: ....

From: ....